BEING SAFE AROUND WATER

DANVILLE PUBLIC LIBRARY
Danville, Indiana

The Child's World

Published by The Child's World®
1980 Lookout Drive • Mankato, MN 56003-1705
800-599-READ • www.childsworld.com

ACKNOWLEDGMENTS
The Child's World®: Mary Berendes, Publishing Director
The Design Lab: Design and production
Red Line Editorial: Editorial direction

LIBRARY OF CONGRESS CATALOGING-IN-PUBLICATION DATA
Kesselring, Susan.
 Being safe around water / by Susan Kesselring;
illustrated by Dan McGeehan.
    p. cm.
 Includes bibliographical references and index.
 ISBN 978-1-60954-298-6 (library bound: alk. paper)
 1. Swimming—Safety measures—Juvenile literature. 2. Aquatic
sports—Safety measures—Juvenile literature. I. McGeehan,
Dan. II. Title.
 GV838.53.S24K47 2011
 797.2'1—dc22   2010040478

Printed in the United States of America
Mankato, MN
December, 2010
PA02069

About the Author
Susan Kesselring loves children, books, nature, and her family. She teaches K-1 students in a progressive charter school down a little country lane in Castle Rock, Minnesota. She is the mother of five daughters and lives in Apple Valley, Minnesota, with her husband, Rob, and a crazy springer spaniel named Lois Lane.

About the Illustrator
Dan McGeehan spent his younger years as an actor, author, playwright, and editor. Now he spends his days drawing, and he is much happier.

W hat's your favorite way to splash? Are you a diver or a water slider? Do you like to ride the ocean's waves? Can you touch the bottom of the pool with your belly? Do you race your canoe across a pond?

Playing around water is a blast! If you follow a few safety rules, you can have tons of fun and still be safe.

3

What's the best way to stay safe around water? Learn to swim! Don't worry if you're not a strong swimmer yet. Ask an adult to teach you how. Or maybe your parents will bring you to swimming lessons. Once you know how to swim, you can play in the deep end.

You can practice your swimming kick. Hold on to the side of the pool. Then float on your belly. Your legs should be at the water's surface. Make small, quick scissor kicks with your legs.

Is a pool your favorite place to swim? Ask your parents how deep you can go. Remember to always have a parent or **lifeguard** watching. Swim with a friend. It's more fun! Plus, you can look out for each other. The **pool deck** can be slippery. Be sure not to run!

There are many types of pools. Some sit on top of the ground. Others are in the ground. Kiddie pools are pretty shallow. They are about one to three feet (.3–.9 m) deep. Swimming pools in the Olympics are huge—164 feet (50 m) long and 82 feet (25 m) wide!

You can't wait to get in the water! Just don't dive headfirst if the water is shallow. You could get seriously hurt. Jump in feet first, and look before you jump. You don't want to land on top of someone.

If you want to dive, ask an adult where it is safe to do so. The water should be at least nine feet (2.7 m) deep.

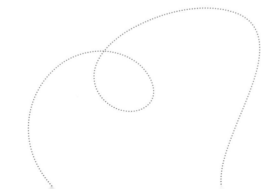

Getting sunburned is no fun. Always wear sunscreen. Rub on more sunscreen after you have been swimming.

9

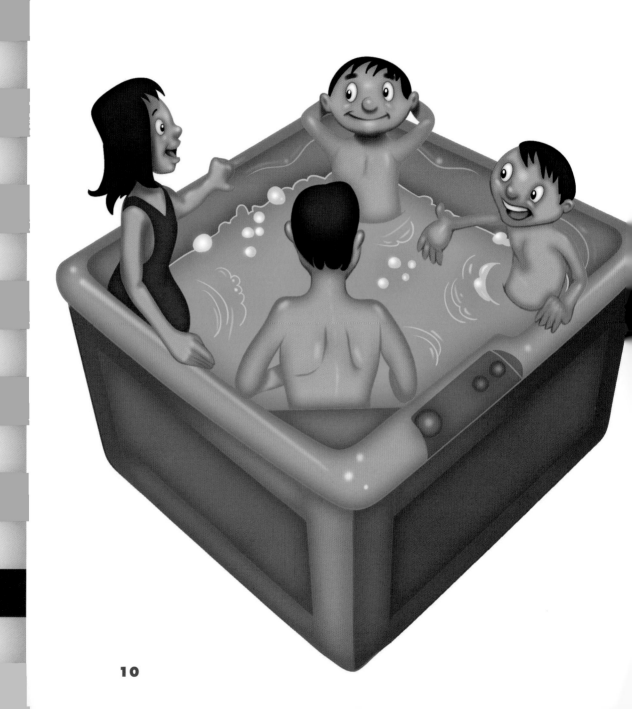

In pools and hot tubs, stay away from the drains on the bottom. Keep food and gum out of your mouth while you are in the water.

The water in hot tubs can be very hot. Have an adult check the temperature and join you in the water. Stay in the water only 20 minutes or less.

Playing at a water park is a whole day's worth of fun! Wear a **life jacket** if you are not a strong swimmer. Always walk to a new ride. And check the rules before you try it. Go down each slide feet first. Make sure a parent or lifeguard is close by, just in case.

Water parks are busy places. What should you do if you lose your parents? Go to one of the workers at the water park and ask for help. If you can't find a worker, find a family. Then ask a parent for help.

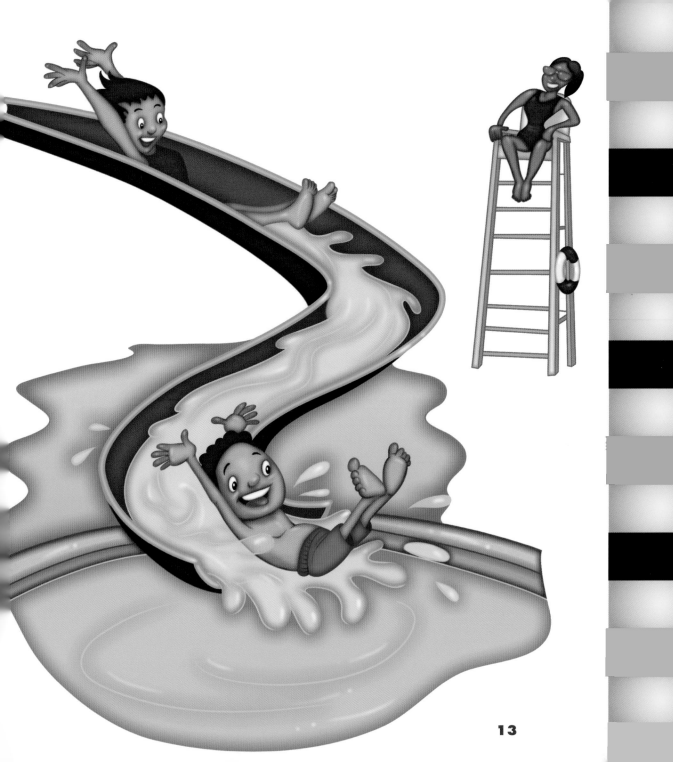

13

14

Swimming in a lake or a river can be tricky. You can't always tell how deep the water is. There could be sharp rocks on the bottom. Wear water shoes to protect your feet. Stay away from very weedy spots that might trap your legs and arms. And always swim with an adult.

Oceans have strong waves and **currents**. These can be strong enough to pull you out into deep water. Have your parents check when the currents are too strong to swim. To stay safe, swim where a lifeguard is watching you. Face the waves so you can see them coming. And always swim with a buddy.

If you see jellyfish, stay away. They can sting!

For beach fun, build your own sand castle. You need wet sand and a small shovel. Start by digging a hole in the sand near the water. You'll soon reach water. Use the wet sand from the hole for building.

How fast can you paddle a canoe? Have you ever ridden in a kayak or a motorboat? It's so much fun to zip over the water.

Whenever you are on a boat, wear a life jacket that is **snug** on your body. If you fall in, you'll float! Stay sitting while your boat is gliding along so you don't tip.

Now you know how to be safe in pools, hot tubs, water parks, rivers, lakes, and oceans.

Here's one last tip for any kind of water play. Do you hear thunder rumbling? Is a storm on its way? Get out of the water right away! If you are boating, get to shore quickly. Take shelter in a car or a building.

Stay out of the water during a thunderstorm. Lightning is electricity. Electricity travels easily through water. It could give you a bad electric **shock**.

WATER SAFETY RULES TO REMEMBER

Always be safe!

1. Have an adult watch you when you are in or near water.

2. Learn to swim well.

3. Always swim with a buddy.

4. Walk around pools and in water parks.

5. Dive only in water that is at least nine feet (2.7 m) deep. If a sign says, "No diving," follow that rule.

6. When boating, always wear a life jacket.

GLOSSARY

currents (KUR-unts): Currents are strong flows of water going one way, most often in rivers or oceans. Ocean currents can pull you out over your head.

lifeguard (LYF-gard): A lifeguard is a person who can rescue swimmers who need help. When swimming in the ocean, make sure a lifeguard is present.

life jacket (LYF JAK-it): A life jacket is a vest filled with material that floats. A life jacket saves you from drowning.

pool deck (POOL DEK): A pool deck is the flat area around the pool. Always walk—don't run—on the pool deck.

shock (SHOK): A shock is the passing of electricity through someone's body. If someone is hit by lightning, he or she would receive a shock.

snug (SNUG): If something is snug, it fits not too tightly and not too loosely. A life jacket should be snug on your body.

TO LEARN MORE

BOOKS

Llewellyn, Claire. *Watch Out! Near Water*. Hauppauge, New York: Barron's Educational Series, 2006.

Pendziwol, Jean E. *A Treasure at Sea for Dragon and Me: Water Safety for Kids (and Dragons)*. Toronto: Kids Can Press, 2005.

Rau, Dana Meachen. *Water Safety*. New York: Marshall Cavendish Benchmark, 2009.

WEB SITES

Visit our Web site for links about being safe around water:
childsworld.com/links

Note to Parents, Teachers, and Librarians: We routinely verify our Web links to make sure they are safe and active sites. So encourage your readers to check them out!